As Clear as It's Ever Been

poems

Peter Jastermsky

It's been a long time since I've been me.
- *Fernando Pessoa*

1.

self-reveal
every limb
trembling

somewhere in his smile the first time he saw her

with great care
the arm
is set down

finding its groove
a voice whispers

"let's get lost - -"

ho w we fir st t ouch af te r no ons try st ing wit h boo ks

closing the blinds
she slips into bed

a sigh . . .

the sound of snaps
undone
one by one

s il k paj am as so fte nin g h er r oug h p atc h

lover's teapot
the slow curve of her handle
in his hand

s udd en m elt a p art ing of t hig hs

she

says

   a hard
left

w here you

feel like

 you can just

k e e p g o i n g

her first time over a paper moon

night train
coupling in sleep
makes it easy

summer

    time
we
 spent

outside

of
time

goo d
    ness

of f it

our bod ies

in
    &
out
of
the

w in d ow
f r a m e

okay
if you
leave

ok
  if

  you bring

back

   breakfast too

lipstick traces
the slow grind
of a jukebox embrace

hearing her sing in a dream a little dream of me

flo
ati
ng

over

our back

  yard   piano

  notes   air
from   her

2.

sleepless . . .
the Titanic
he sinks into

the mysteries of space
she hands him a map
of Utah

this is just
to say

you're no
ripe plum

your
self

we've all been here
a rustle of clothing
in the dark

a muffled curse
acting as if

everything's fine

pul ling aw ay it s par tly yo ur fau lt li ne

mor.
ning

rep
ast

a me
mory

t h e l e n g t h

of
   our

l a
  st

    v / o / l / l / e / y

ats uch spe eda st obeb e we il de red

going back on her word for a shorter one

scented soap
why should I
believe you

cro ssi ng th e fie ld t hat fe nce we nev er g et o ver

he hadn't drawn a blank until

last anniversary
the secret password
they once had for love

in her place a thousand angry bees

of all
the joys
I have

lost

now
you

how she once
whispered
every request

bossa nova
to samba

saudade

3.

chalk mandala
in short
the wind

doing the aftermath

ven
hea
new
the
now
les
ho
bit
rab

alone in bed

after all
these years

the first time
seeing himself
as hungry

the moon floats down
sits on a park bench
and listens

it's the middle of a workday
no one notices

a young girl approaches
and circles the bench

I'm pretending to be
a satellite, she says

what are you
pretending to be

a moon
with no

words for
wounded

in a box marked fragile the pit of his stomach

remembering
her silence

remembering

how
snow
falls

          pin drop
          morning

          the last
          good hinge

          on door
          number one

               **

          dividing up
          what has

          been shared
          that line

          the sand is
          so sick of

               **

          new worries
          a barn beam

          tunneled
          by termites

          the shape
          of karma

               **

gum wrapper chain
when was there
that much time

off in the distance my adult children again child size

surrounded

    by   horseshoe

  crabs

  age

  eight

forever

thirty years

a chasm too wide
to jump

memory lane
deadends
at the junkyard

at the end of this sentence our blue period

der
pon
to
sky
the
for
it
   ving
lea

muted melancholy

the horn player's
sketches of Spain

playing
to moonlit
shadows

weighing a response
the eggshells
in her email

another trip down
If Only
Boulevard

as if
this time

we'll stay in synch

do not refreeze
the afterburn
of single-size portions

family photo
a hole punch
of all things

unlit candle
it could've been
a contender

so much depends on the strength of teabags

n o

  C o n

T a
C t

a l
M o
s T

  c r   i   c K   e t   S

tiptoeing
 around

the first
fallen

 leaves
only

humans
worry

about
dying

re
mo vi   fr
 ng   ee

    my

      fa
      ll
the   ot
    her s

rin   ha
    lf

g

morning again the rocks I've already rolled

s__
k_ng

tr_ns   c_nd_

     nc_

t h_   _mp

     _st_r

synd

r_m_

     O   k_y

f_
    r n_

w

4.

approaching stillness
one monkey mind
remains

begin again. white whiskers in the sink. all the time in the world.

The Measure of Days

five addresses ago
who were we?

    just the lips of air moving

the voices of people
from anywhere but here

    a soloing bird *"ne quitte pas"*?

morning settles into
a playground swing

intermittent sun needing a push

the measure of days
a bean can's rust line

love thy neighbor speculating wildly

how unknowing turns
to ninja in our hands

what comes after *so long*

we each have our way
of finding
the light

in the first available
hello

greeting a stranger we compare hands before words

on her lashes a fellow particle of strangeness

in the wee small hours

a singer lost
in lamplight

hands
over
his foolish heart

f nDng

there

'S

Not

h Ng

m s s n g

tucked inside
the morning

laughs
chuckles

grins
groans

smiles
that make

their own
sound

rewriting the rules
to see
what happens . . .

around the corner
a couple flirts

with nakedness

over a plate of grapes the lovers found waltzing

in
the

0
of

her
mouth

room
to

draw
down

the
moon

less
the
none
soar
I will
ghts
hei-
of
afraid
dom
free
but
ing
noth
ing
know
flies
a bird
house
the
over

across a mountain half hidden in haze this life as clear as it's ever been

ACKNOWLEDGEMENTS

My grateful thanks to the editors of the following publications in which present or earlier versions of some of these poems first appeared:

Cold Moon Journal, Failed Haiku, MacQueen's Quinterly, Password: the journal of very short poetry, Poetry Pea Journal, Puddock, The Cherita and Under the Basho